The Dog Who Couldn't Bark

BY LEILA KOZAK

ILLUSTRATED BY KRISDIANI SUNDARI

THE DOG WHO COULDN'T BARK

For more information contact the author at:
leila@inspiringrelationship.org

ISBN: 979-8-4822090-5-9

First Edition: September 2021

DEDICATION

For Dippy, to your love for kids and dogs and your legacy in transforming early childhood education.

To Charlie and Henry, our furry "love teachers" and Jasmine, who brought these four-legged love teachers into our lives.

To Paul, who understood how to connect with the pure love that these love teachers radiated.

To our 6 grandkids: Naomi, Henry the boy, Akemi, Violet, Eleanor and Orlando - who brought even more love back to the little love teachers.

TABLE OF CONTENTS

CHAPTER 1

Mom, can we get a dog?"

Leila looked up from her computer. "No, Jasmine. Dogs are too much work. I am not sure we can take care of a dog at this time."

Ten-year-old Jasmine gave her best pleading look. "Mom, can we get a dog? I want a dog to play with."

Jasmine was an only child, and Leila really wanted her to have a dog for a friend. Life just seemed too busy to care for a dog. Secretly, Leila had always wanted a dog, too. The problem was, she would need to give the dog a good doggie life and she was not sure she could do that.

Days later, Jasmine tried again. "Mom, can we get a dog? I want a dog to play with."

Leila shook her head. "No, Jasmine. Dogs are too much work. Who is going to walk the dog? Feed the dog? Bathe the dog? Play with the dog while you are school?

"Dogs depend on us. It is a big job to have a dog. You have to think about how you will take care of the dog. You can't return the dog if it is too much work. Besides, I have never had a dog before, so there may be other things I don't know that could be even more work… "

Jasmine really wanted a dog. Days later, she was still thinking how to convince her mom to get a dog. She was not going to give up! She imagined how happy she would be playing with her dog.

Mom always said, "Do not take a no for an answer!" Well, she was just practicing what mom taught her. Maybe if she just insisted a little more… She kept thinking what the best way would be to convince her mom. There had to be a way.

The next day, Jasmine had a great idea. It was

time to try again. “Mom, do you remember how you told me that dogs are a lot of work?”

“Yes, Jasmine. I believe they are a lot of work,” Leila said.

“Well, I also heard you saying that you have never had a dog before… is that true?” Jasmine asked. She was excited about her brilliant argument…

"Yes, it is true. I have never had a dog because my family always said that dogs were too much work," Leila said. She was worried about where Jasmine was going with this...

"Well, the thing is… if you have never had a dog, how do you know that dogs are too much work? Aren't you a scientist? You taught me that scientists look for evidence. Scientists are not supposed to believe something to be true unless they find the evidence first. How are you going to find the evidence that a dog is too much work if you have never had a dog?"

Ooops, thought Leila, she is right! Caught by Jasmine's clever argument, Leila had to agree. "You are right, darling. I guess we will have to explore the evidence first. Moms can always be wrong..."

As if she was not already making her point clear, Jasmine gave her mom some extra convincing arguments. “Besides that, I think you’d really like having a dog. Dogs are fluffy. They like to cuddle and they are so loyal! I know you like fluffy, cuddly and loyal so I am sure you would love a dog!

“Dogs love their humans and they always want to play. I want a dog to play with!” Jasmine was getting more and more excited as she watched her words convince her mom!

Leila shook her head. “I guess we will have to do some research about dogs...

CHAPTER 2

Jasmine was excited! She might actually get that dog she so much wanted. Maybe mom was right. Don't take a no for an answer.

The next day, Jasmine went to school all excited and thinking about the dog. She wondered how she and her mom could take care of this "dog research" business. Was it possible they could find a dog that they could try? She would have to find a way to see how much work it really was to have a dog.

Jasmine had to do a school project about something she was excited about. Of course the project would be about dogs! Jasmine went to her computer to learn everything there was to know about dogs.

She learned that there are many different dog breeds. Different dog breeds can have very different needs.

Some breeds, like German Shepherds, tend to act like protectors or guardian dogs. Other breeds may enjoy being trained for other jobs. For example, Australian shepherd dogs like herding sheep. Beagles help humans in hunting. Other dogs are lap dogs that love lying around on their humans' laps. Small Maltese dogs are like that.

Jasmine learned that some dogs have fur while others have hair just like people. This can make a big difference for people who have allergies or asthma. The dogs that have hair instead of fur are called non-shedding dogs. Their hair does not shed and they are a perfect match for people with allergy or asthma. Some non-shedding breeds are Bichon Frises, Poodles and Maltese.

There are dogs that are a mix of shedding and non-shedding breeds, like Goldendoodles. They are a mix of Golden Retrievers and Poodles. Sometimes these mix dogs are also non-shedding and oh, so cute!!!

Jasmine knew that before they adopted a dog, they would need to learn what type of dog was best for their family. She read that some large dog breeds and puppies need a lot of exercise. They are best for people who go running with their dogs or who can spend at least an hour a day each day walking the dog. Some small breeds and older dogs may only need 30-minute walks.

Then Jasmine learned that there were lots of dogs waiting to be adopted at shelter and rescue organizations. Rescue organizations are groups of people who care a lot about animals. They take in animals who don't have owners or were abandoned.

Sometimes they take in puppies and give them to people who can take care of them. Some rescues have a place where they keep the dogs until someone adopts them. Other times, the dogs are kept at "foster homes" where people take care of the dogs (or cats) until someone can adopt the animal forever.

Jasmine learned about people who breed dogs and don't treat them well. These people have many dogs but they don't love the dogs. They just breed them to sell the puppies. They are call "puppy mills." Not all puppies come from puppy mills. Some people feel strongly that getting dogs from shelters or rescues is a better choice than buying puppies. There are so many dogs that don't have a home!

Jasmine felt so sad about this that she decided her new dog would be adopted from a shelter or a rescue.

The research paid off. Not only did Jasmine get an excellent grade in her project, but she was also now an expert on how to search for the perfect dog!

That day, Jasmine came home from school thinking of all the new dog facts she was going to share with her mom. She thought about her next move. How could she bring in a dog to try without actually adopting a dog? Maybe her mom would agree to foster a dog! But that would take longer that she wanted to wait.

Then she remembered something. For their last family vacation her family rented a car. When her mom picked out the car at the rental place, she said she wanted to try that car because she might want to buy one herself. She thought renting the car would be a great way to try it out. Jasmine's face lit up with excitement at her brilliant idea.

"Mama, can we rent a dog?" Jasmine asked as soon as she got home. "Mama, let's rent a dog so we can try it. Please!!!"

Leila laughed. "No Jasmine, dogs can't be rented out, they are living creatures, just like people. But I think that you have a great idea. Maybe we can borrow a dog. We can ask the neighbor when they go on vacation if we can take care of their dog. We'll call it a "summer dog rental!"

Summer was just around the corner and people go away on vacation. Many people can't take their dogs on their vacation. So when the neighbor announced they were going on a two-week vacation, Leila offered to take care of their dog while they were away. It was a perfect solution: happy neighbors, happy dog and happy Jasmine.

Well, so they thought…

CHAPTER 3

They "rented" the black lab for two weeks. He was super sweet, but, wow, the black lab was a lot of dog. He ate a lot. He shed a lot. He ran a lot. When Jasmine walked him, she had to walk a lot.

Besides, the dog was so big and strong that when Jasmine walked the dog… well, it was more like the dog walked Jasmine instead. He pulled so hard that Jasmine could barely stay on the sidewalk. She looked like a kite flying on the leash, propelled by the dog.

The black lab was playful and adorable, and he was a handful. For two weeks, they picked him up at his home every morning and returned him every evening so he could sleep at his home. The neighbors knew he had a bit of separation anxiety. They were concerned about letting the dog sleep in somebody's else home.

The first day Jasmine thought they were exaggerating. But when she came over the next morning to pick up the sweet dog, she saw the way he had ripped apart his bed.

He scattered all the inside filling and destroyed every pillow on the sofas. He missed his family very much.

One day the dog got muddy and Jasmine had to wash him. Washing the dog was an adventure. He did not fit in the small shower. He was too heavy to pick up and put in the bathtub. Jasmine tried using a hose outside on the deck. After all, it was summer!

The dog left some of his fur wherever she sat with him. Jasmine, Paul and Leila found out they were allergic to dog fur. They had sneezing contests!

The two weeks passed and the black lab returned to his loving and understanding owners. Leila said to Jasmine, "Thank you for your great idea. I guess no black labs for our family, huh?"

Jasmine agreed. She thought, "At least now we are seeing eye to eye…"

After the lab went back home, Leila said, "I think we should research smaller dogs."

"How about a Bichon Frise or a miniature poodle?" Jasmine asked. After her school project, she was an expert on dog breeds. "They don't shed, they weigh about seven times less than a lab, and they are lap dogs. And they would fit in our kitchen sink when they need a bath! Mama please, can we find one of these?"

Leila looked up. "Okay, Jasmine, let's get a dog!"

CHAPTER 4

Jasmine was eager to pick out her dog right away.

They heard there was a pet adoption event on Saturday at the local park.

Jasmine said, "Let's go!"

Jasmine and Leila walked into the park's playground area. The rescue organization had set up tents to shelter people and dogs from the summer sun. They put up barriers so the dogs and kids would not run away.

At the pet adoption event there were lots of dogs and people playing with them. Dogs were everywhere! Big dogs, small dogs, black dogs, white dogs, friendly dogs, shy dogs, dogs, dogs, dogs! Jasmine sat down on the ground so she could pet some of the dogs.

Suddenly, a little all-white Bichon and Maltese

mix dog jumped into Jasmine's lap! Jasmine smiled and giggled as the "Maltichon" (the name for a mix Bichon and Maltese) licked her face and sat on her lap. "This is the one, Mom!" Jasmine said. "I'm going to name him Charlie!" It was love at the first lick!

Jasmine wanted to take him right home, but they already had a trip scheduled to visit Jasmine's grandmom in Buenos Aires, Argentina. Leila said, "First we're flying to Argentina to visit your abuela. We we'll apply to adopt Charlie. If the rescue people think we are a good family for him, we will adopt him as soon as we get back."

Jasmine rubbed Charlie's tummy. She said, "I really hope in a couple weeks you get to come home with me!"

Jasmine chattered about Charlie during the whole trip to Argentina. As it turned out, the rescue people thought that Jasmine's family was a great fit for Charlie and they received a notice saying that the adoption was approved.

Finally, the day came to pick him up. Leila and Jasmine drove to Seattle, about 30 minutes away from their home, to pick up Charlie. He was living with his doggie foster care mom.

Leila and Jasmine walked into the house where

Charlie was living. The little ten-pound bundle of energy was even cuter than Jasmine remembered. Charlie barked like he remembered Jasmine, too.

Then the doggie foster care mom said, “Charlie has a friend.” She pointed out another Poodle/Bichon Frise mix dog (also known as “Poochons”). With his short peach and white curly hair he looked just like a stuffed animal. “This is Henry. Please, can you take them both? They will be so sad if they have to leave each other. Charlie and Henry both came from the same high-kill shelter. They traveled together from the shelter and they became very close friends.”

“A high kill shelter?” Jasmine asked. “What’s that?”

The foster mom explained, “A high-kill shelter is a place where they don’t have enough space for all the dogs. People may not adopt the dogs as fast as they come in. Because they don’t have enough space and resources to care for the dogs, they have to kill some dogs to have space for others.

"Many rescue organizations work with volunteers at those shelters. They tell them how these dogs are in danger to be killed soon. The rescue organizations take them in and save their lives. Then they bring the dogs to foster homes, so people like you can adopt them,"

Jasmine and Leila were speechless and tearful.

They had no idea what so many dogs had to go through. Leila said, “I was only planning to get one dog, not two! But I can’t bear to separate them... We are taking both dogs home with us.”

Leila and Jasmine drove back home with two new furry friends.

The rescued dogs were finally home!

CHAPTER 5

When they walked in the door, the dogs went straight for Paul. He bent down and scratched them in all the right places. Jasmine asked, "How did you know how to do that?"

Paul said, "I was raised on a farm with farm dogs!" He rubbed Henry's tummy.

Leila said, "Let's get them something to eat!" She got out the chicken dog food she had bought from the store.

Charlie and Henry didn't touch it.

"Maybe try a different type of dog food," Paul suggested.

Leila bought doggie beef food. No luck. Then she bought food with grains. She bought food without grains. She bought food in small morsels for little mouths. She even bought fancy salmon kibble. The dogs would not eat. Leila was starting to get worried

Paul made fun of her. "You don't need to worry about dogs not eating. They will eat when they are hungry enough. Besides, they are still stressed out because of the many home changes they just went through. They will be fine. You will see."

Paul grew up with dogs, so Leila trusted his advice. Still, seeing those little fluff balls not eating for days broke her mama's heart.

That night at dinner Jasmine accidentally dropped one of her favorite meatballs from Costco on the floor.

"Woof!" Charlie ate the meatball.

"Look at that!" Leila said. "Drop another one!"

Henry gobbled it up.

Henry and Charlie loved Costco meatballs! They couldn't get enough of them! The dogs went crazy over Costco meatballs! Leila went back to Costco and she bought more meatballs.

In time, the dogs learned to love other foods as well. Although Costco meatballs were always a favorite treat. Charlie was kind of a roasted chicken type of guy. Henry liked avocados and many types of fruit. He really loved apples, but only if they were juicy and sweet, combined with a bit of tartness. No bland apples for this canine connoisseur!

CHAPTER 6

Jasmine, Leila and Paul quickly learned that Charlie was an expert barker. The white fluff ball was ten pounds of barking muscle!

He barked at home, he barked at the park, he barked in the car, he barked at the door. He took his job as mini-guard dog very seriously. He barked at dogs, he barked at visitors, he barked to get petted and he barked when petting stopped. Charlie barked enough for two dogs!

Henry did not bark, ever. He didn't know how!

So he let Charlie do all the barking, which was just fine with Charlie. Instead of barking, Henry used his eyes and sometimes his paws or his wet little nose.

One day Leila was working hard at her computer. Henry came in for some petting. He tried to make eye contact with her. That didn't work, so he touched her legs with his paws and his wet nose. Leila was concentrating so hard she didn't notice. Then, Henry gently licked her ankle with his little wet tongue.

Jasmine watched Henry. She said, "Mom! Henry wants a pet!"

Leila looked down at Henry. He seemed to be saying, "Come on, Mama, I tried my eyes and paws! I even licked your ankle! Do I need to scratch your leg to get a pet? What are you waiting for? I need a rub!"

Leila couldn't resist those deep brown eyes. She got up from her computer and sat down on the sofa. Henry snuggled in closer and closer until he rested his head on her warm lap. When Leila started petting his head and neck, he rolled over, legs up, and looked into her eyes.

Jasmine said, "I know what he's saying! 'Time to rub my belly, Mama! More, more, more!'"

"I think you're exactly right," Leila said, and she gave Henry a nice long belly rub.

Since Paul knew all about dogs from his farm days, he took on training Charlie and Henry "all the good stuff." He taught them doggie games, how to go out the doggie door and how to come back inside for treats. He played hide-and-seek in the house with them, hiding behind the doors and whistling at them so they could find him. He rubbed Charlie and Henry's bellies until someone got tired, usually Paul.

Henry was so quiet that Jasmine thought he didn't have a voice. But one day Paul was howling with Charlie, "Oooooooooo," and Henry wanted in on the fun! He suddenly joined the duo and then there were three guys singing happily to the howling tune! But Henry still did not bark.

CHAPTER 7

The years went by. Jasmine grew up and moved away, and Henry and Charlie grew old in dog years. Henry's back hurt him sometimes.

He still loved his walks, but he could no longer make it a whole walk without getting tired. He stopped and looked up at Paul as if to say, "Papa, please carry me." And Paul picked him up and carried him for the rest of the walk.

When Henry could no longer jump up on the sofa, Paul or Leila would pick him up and lift him to his favorite spot. They were worried that he would hurt himself when he tried to get down, so they surrounded him with pillows.

Paul asked Leila, “What if Henry wants to get off the sofa and we’re not in the room to help him? I’m going to teach him how to bark so he can ask for help.”

So Paul started teaching the old dog a new trick. First, Paul stacked pillows in front of the couch so Henry couldn’t jump off by himself. Then he pretended to leave the room when Henry was on the couch. Paul hid behind the couch and softly whistled for Henry. Henry, seeing he had no way to get off the couch made the softest little "r r r" sound.

Paul immediately came from behind the couch. He told Henry he was a good boy and gave him his favorite snack. Then he picked him up and set him on the floor. Henry was so excited to be off the couch he ran off to find Charlie and Leila.

Paul did this again and again, each time waiting a little longer so Henry had to make a louder noise before getting him off the couch. One day Henry made a sound that almost sounded like a "r r r-woof!" Paul gave Henry two snacks and a big pat on his head. Henry quickly learned that if he "woofed" louder, Paul would come sooner.

One day, Paul forgot Henry was on the couch all by himself and he went to the back of the house. Suddenly, Paul heard this very loud bark! Then he heard it again! It was Henry telling him to come get him off the couch. Henry no longer "woofed," he had learned to bark!

Henry was 14 years old when he finally learned how to bark. His bark sounded like a low woof-wooooof. Leila laughed and cried as she listened. “He’s so cute! After 14 years of silence, he can bark!”

Henry liked his new little bark. Charlie was also old and a little bit deaf, so he didn’t always hear when there was someone at the door. Henry helped out by giving a couple of low “woof’s” when someone rang the doorbell.

Then one year Henry got very sick and Paul and Leila thought they were going to lose him, but he recovered. Henry lived for two more years, loving Paul and Leila with the same boundless love he'd shared with them his whole life.

And then, when Henry was 16 years old, he left this earth to go to doggie heaven. Leila, Paul, Jasmine and Charlie were very, very sad. They were comforted when they imagined Henry running free, jumping and dancing and playing and enjoying the sound of his newfound "woof" forever.

ACKNOWLEDGMENTS

With deep appreciation for the gifts of Donna McFarland (spencermeadowpress.com), who edited the transcript and designed the book, and Krisdiani Sundari (instagram: @kirdianis), whose soulful illustrations made the story come alive.

PHOTO ALBUM

Leila with Henry and Charlie

Henry

www.ingramcontent.com/pod-product-compliance
Lightning Source LLC
LaVergne TN
LVHW020523160826
845677LV00015B/3873

* 9 7 9 8 4 8 2 2 0 9 0 5 9 *